I Wake-Up Beautiful . . .

And Other Fantasies

by

Mary E. Hirsch

D1265333

Swell Gal   Minneapolis, MN

First Edition 2000
Second Printing

Printed in Canada

Library of Congress Catalog Number: 00 090645

Hirsch, Mary E.

I Wake-Up Beautiful . . . And Other Fantasies
Summary: A collection of humor essays and cartoons

Portions of this book were previously published, in whole or in part, in issues of the *Southwest Journal*, Minneapolis, Minnesota and the *Minnesota Women's Press,* St. Paul, Minnesota and are reprinted with permission of both publications.

ISBN: 0-9701812-0-5

This Book is dedicated to my Girl Scout
Troop No. 1792:

Maggie Barnick
Cami Czech
Sarah Heil
Amanda Hernandez
Amanda Jordi
Suzie Ivkovic
Katie Jubert
Heather Rewey
Katelyn Saiko
Britty Ukestad
Kathy Xu

and my favorite Brownie Megan Saiko.

Dream big dreams
Girls Rock!!!!

And, as always, to Britta, Perry and Brett Hirsch
who put up with their eccentric Aunt and always
make her laugh.

Table of Contents

"Some mornings it's a challenge to decide whether to stay in bed or get up and create havoc in the world."

I Wake-Up Beautiful

Every day when I arise,
No cellulite jiggles on my thighs,
And no puffiness lurks beneath my eyes,
For I wake-up beautiful.

My hair is clean and right in place,
You'll find no wrinkle in my nightie's lace,
And a healthy glow beams from my face,
For I wake-up beautiful.

My voice is golden, it never cracks,
On my teeth there is no trace of plaque,
And I alight delicately from the sack,
For I wake-up beautiful.

My breath is fresh as morning rain,
My body feels no twinge of pain,
And never a pound have I gained,
For I wake-up beautiful.

My pillowcase is free of drool,
I don't perspire — my pits are cool,
And no scent rises from my stools,
For I wake-up beautiful.

My pores are healthy — opened wide,
My nostrils are all clean inside,
And no make-up need I apply,
For I wake-up beautiful.

Mary E. Hirsch

My skin is taunt, it does not sag,
My buttock's high, it doesn't drag,
And no unwanted hairs are on my legs,
For I wake-up beautiful.

My fingernails are strong and gleaming,
My rosy cheeks are simply beaming,
And my entire existence is redeeming,
For I wake-up beautiful.

My skin's so smooth, it has no wrinkles,
My eyes sparkle with a loving twinkle,
And I never have to rush to tinkle,
For I wake-up beautiful.

For me each new day dawns so bright,
Because I always look just right,
Let's be honest, I'm a sheer delight,
For I wake-up beautiful.

JESSE'S GIRL
A MINNESOTAN REFLECTS ON HER GOVERNOR

I was born in Minnesota and have lived here all my life. It use to be when I'd travel and tell people where I'm from they always had one of three responses: "What do you raise on your farm?"; "Don't you get awfully cold?"; or "Do you know Prince?" I usually tell them Prince use to work on my icicle farm, which would cover all three questions in one quick answer. But today if I tell them I'm from Minnesota I get one response "Oh yeah, your governor is Jesse Ventura isn't he?" that is followed by a look that says "Hey do you know your standing in dog poop?"

So my governor is a celebrity. When was the last time you turned on Letterman and saw the governor of Iowa or Idaho or any of the other states? Sure he use to wear a boa, but how many of us can honestly say we haven't worn one too (at least in the privacy of our own homes)? And yes it's true he wants to be reincarnated as a large bra, but would it make him a better person if he said he wanted to come back as a plaid flannel nightie, a sweatshirt or anything by Ralph Lauren?

At first it didn't endear Ventura to me when he warned Minnesotans about tourists by telling us "If you see people walking around and they're staring at you, they're not doing it to be rude. They want to see who it was who elected me." It's akin to being the bearded lady in the carnival sideshow. "Step right up and see the freak of nature who cast a ballot electing Jesse "The Body" Ventura as Governor of Minnesota. She walks, she talks, she makes sculptures out of Spam." Then I realized what a big favor

9

he had done by taking a lot of pressure off of Minnesotans because now we know that people are only staring at us because they think we voted for Ventura, not because there's a booger hanging from our nose, our fly is open or a piece of dental floss is stuck to our chin.

Some people from Minnesota are embarrassed by Ventura, some are enthralled, but most are like me and think of him as an amusing, eccentric relative — my Uncle Jesse. He says whatever he wants, he's pretty harmless, and he can kick the ass of everyone else's uncles. You want him to show up at family functions, but you'd rather not have him come and live with you. And that is what people who talk about Uncle Jesse, I mean Governor Ventura, running for president need to remember.

Sure we may all be frozen farmers who live next door to Prince, but Minnesotans know the difference between a joke and a potential disaster. As governor, Jesse is amusing and quaint (or as quaint as a giant, bald headed, former pro wrestler can be); as president Jesse is ridiculous! And that is why Minnesotans are starting to stare at nonresidents who want to elect Ventura for president — it's not that we're being rude, we just want to see who it is that has their heads up their butts.

MARY E. HIRSCH

How Functional Are Your Foods?

A recent issue of the Minneapolis' *CityBusiness* had a story about Lynn Gordon, president of French Meadow Bakery. Actually the story was about her new line of breads called "Woman's Bread." At first I thought it was called that because it only cost 60% of what a man's bread cost and once a month it got bloated, but that wasn't the case. It was created to help women cope naturally with menopause and PMS using soy protein, fiber and cranberries. One can only hope that some day there will be a product that copes with menopause and PMS using chocolate, marshmallows, and whipped creme — but until that day we have this concoction to help us along.

For some odd reason *CityBusiness* felt is was important to talk to Scott Schwartz, a Brooklyn Park entrepreneur, about Gordon's new product. Schwartz said "Targeting women will limit the sales of the product. I think it will alienate half the population. The benefits to men will be overlooked if it's called 'Woman's Bread.'" Duh! This from someone who is developing a "functional coffee" that he says will relieve symptoms of PMS. Unless it will relieve the symptoms of men complaining about women having PMS I think his coffee may also have limited sales.

Apparently Gordon was not aware of this limitation. She said she was looking for "a healthful food alternative to estrogen replacement therapy" when she started developing this bread. Perhaps she could come up with a loaf of bread that is a healthful food alternative to Viagra and Rogaine. Add a dash of beer, find a way to toast it using a remote control, put a super model on the wrapper, and you'd have the perfect man's bread.

Woman's Bread is part of a growing industry called "functional foods." Oh goodie, not only do we have to read the label to be sure our food is low fat, low sodium, low calorie, high protein, high calcium, high fiber, organic, free range, minimal packaging, all natural, doesn't harm the ozone layer, rain forests, or ecosystem, and proceeds go to save the dolphins, cure a disease, or Jerry's kids, we now have to find out if it is a functional food. I have looked in my own cupboards and refrigerator to see what foods I have, and try to figure out what is their function.

Frozen ears of corn. Their function as far as I can tell is to force you to floss your teeth.

Three jars of pickles, each with about one pickle left in it. I think their function is to help me deal with my inability to finish projects I've started.

An unopened box of Grape Nuts that is about three years old. Its function is to taunt my colon every time I open the cupboard and see it. I can almost hear my optic nerves alert my brain to send a false message of hope to my digestive system.

An orange (or it could be a tangerine) shriveled up and rolling around my produce bin. Its function is to remind me to put on some skin creme.

A can of Spaghettios that I usually eat cold, out of the can. This allows me to fantasize that I am either a backpacker climbing Mt. Everest, or a frat boy eating another gourmet meal.

A box of frozen veggie burgers remind me of good intentions and is an excellent place to stack pints of ice cream.

HoHos are really metaphors for our need to laugh at ourselves.

Twinkies are really metaphors for our need to laugh at lawyers.

UFO (Unknown Frozen Object) wrapped in aluminum foil covered with ice way in the back of the freezer helps us improve our memories as we try to remember just what it was that we stuck back there, and exactly when it was placed there. It also challenges our sense of adventure when we decide whether to consume it or toss it.

Can of Peas remind us of starving children in Europe who would be glad to have a can of peas. (Note: "Can of Peas" is not to be confused with "canapés" that function as little bits of food that you can eat a lot of but not feel like you've eaten a lot because they are so small.) Of course starving children in Europe would like canapés too, but your mother never forced them down your throat.

And as for all those plastic containers filled with who-knows-what covered with green stuff, they can either remind us to go for a walk and enjoy the great green outdoors, or to never do anything that might result in catching something only penicillin will cure.

The Seven Habits Of Highly Guilt-Ridden People

MARY E. HIRSCH

Not Such Precious Moments

I went to a local gift shop the other day to find a birthday card and discovered I had walked in on some kind of Precious Moments new release party. It was a porcelain beanie baby frenzy. For those of you who don't know, Precious Moments are collectible statues of wide-eyed cherubs that have sweet specific themes so you can give them for different occasions. For the golfer there is "Lord Help Me To Stay On The Course"; for the newlyweds there is "I Give You My Love Forever True"; and for a marathon runner there is "Bless Your Sole." But there is nothing for those not so precious moments that you may want to remember. I think I'll start a new line of gift statues called "Not Such Precious Moments" with the following starter figurines:

"Yeah, Sure The Earth Moved For Me" — Yes, yes, yes, yes, you'll love our consummated cuties as they reflect on their first sexual encounter. With close attention to detail you can see the disappointment in their eyes and can almost hear him saying "Sure I still respect you."

"Pounding The Pavement" — There's no downsizing how adorable this out-of-work executive will look in your home (while you still have it). That cute furrowed brow will help you forget all those years of dedicated service and loyalty that earned you a pink slip.

"The Dog Ate My Receipts" — Padded accounts. Fake deductions. The IRS has finally caught up with you. This big-eyed serious auditor will make any tax evader smile through their tears.

"Irreconcilable Differences" — Observe the filing of a final divorce decree with this fine crafted figure of Slick, the family law attorney. With dissolution papers in his left hand, and a bill in his right hand, you just know there are Porsche catalogs in his briefcase.

"Stop And Smell The Clairol" — Our hairstylist Geoffrey is to dye for. A perfect gift for the baby boomer who just discovered the first gray hair. With a little help from a bottle, Geoffrey will wash away your blues as he washes away your grays.

"Go To Hill" — Our quaint quorum of Congressional officials are ready to investigate yet another political scandal. They are so charming you won't be able to resist their questions — and that's the truth, the whole truth, and nothing but the truth (sort of).

"That's Entertainment?????" — The critics warned you. Your gut warned you. Even the person at the ticket window warned you. Now the disappointed look on the face of our morose movie goer will never let you forget your first Pauly Shore movie

"Byte Me" — Your memory will never be insufficient enough to forget the thrill of your first system crash with this figurine of Fred, our favorite frenzied computer nerd. Set it next to your monitor and feel that sense of panic all over again every time you turn on your computer.

"False Advertising" — When your dream date from the personals turns into a nightmare from dating hell, remember it with our date ditching dandy. Seeing this guy

Mary E. Hirsch

(or gal) climbing out the bathroom window will remind you that "good-looking, sophisticated, fun-loving" often means loser!

"There Go My Premiums" — The memories will pile-up every time you look at this tow truck hauling away a totaled car. You will vividly recall squealing tires, shattering tail lights, bending metal and the feeling of camaraderie as everyone exchanges insurance information in the glow of flashing red lights.

"Strangers In The Shower" — All you'll be wearing is a smile when you look at the newest member of the Not So Precious Moments Health Club experiencing her first group shower. The handpainted blush is so real you may say out loud "Why don't they make bigger wash cloths?"

"Let Me See Your License and Registration" — You can't help but get caught laughing at Cletus, our tough little State Patrol officer. With an oversized hat and a book of speeding tickets in his hand it will be radar love at first sight. Just the happy reminder we all need of speeding tickets gone by.

"*(#*#$&()@" — Our mopish little towhead is just the thing to remember that day when you said those fateful words "I just want a trim." This dorky little dickens will grow on you as you grow out your do.

"Would You Like Fries With That?" — When counter culture means you're working the lunch shift at the local fast food bistro, our lovable drive-thru clerk will super size your heart.

"Free Clinic" — When the love bug has bitten, our Free Clinic figurine will be just the booster shot you'll need. Put Bertha the County Health Nurse on your coffee table and you can almost smell the antiseptic swabs.

And remember, if you buy three or more Not So Precious Moment statues we'll throw in for free our Not So Precious Moment Christmas Ornament "What Do You Mean I'm Over My Credit Limit?"

MARY E. HIRSCH

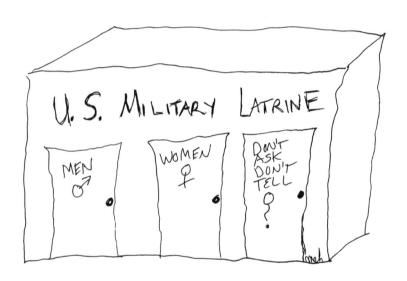

If They Don't Ask; Don't Tell

Every day we are put into situations where we could begin or get drawn into a casual conversation with a total stranger. You chat with the person behind you in the line at the grocery store; you have a few words about the weather with the bank teller; or you find yourself sharing a bus seat with someone who is telling you about his recent trip to the Planet Snagtzborg.

Chatting is a friendly, neighborly kind of thing to do. But if you should find yourself in a casual conversation, it's wise to use discretion in what you share with that other person because it may not be kept in confidence. If you are in doubt about what is appropriate to share, and what is not wise to share, here are some secrets it is best to keep to yourself:

- You have good reason to believe that Martha Stewart is really Elvis.

- Road construction is your favorite part of summer.

- You once won a sixth-grade poetry contest by plagiarizing a Rod McKuen poem.

- You have a tatoo of Henry Kissinger somewhere on your body.

- The tie you are wearing was once worn by Jerry Lewis.

- You think the government should use funds to buy accordions for underprivileged children.

Mary E. Hirsch

- Every time you hear Barry Manilow sing "Mandy" you cry like a baby.

- You have a secret desire to shave your head and dance naked on local cable television.

- A psychic said that in a previous life you were a disease-infested tavern owner.

- Martha Washington is the only woman who ever understood you.

- Your hobby is translating the works of Jackie Collins into Sanskrit.

- You have so much hair on your feet that people think you're wearing fuzzy slippers at the beach.

- When you're feeling a little down you watch A&E's biography of Jerry Vale and it cheers you right up.

- The last good movie you saw was "Biodome."

- Sometimes you can't get to sleep trying to decide between MCI, Sprint and AT&T.

- You've named your teeth.

- You thought the "X Files" was a show about portly people who worked as file clerks.

- You believe Demi Moore has been unjustly overlooked by the Academy Awards.

- You'd seen "Evita" three times before you realized it was a musical.

- When this CD fad blows over you are sure 8-tracks will come back into style.

- You are working in your basement to find a way to clone Sara Lee.

- If you were elected President of the United States you would make everyone change their name to Wally.

- Your idea of a fun Saturday night is to give yourself a good dental flossing and gum massage.

- You like to sleep in your bowling shirt.

- If there is such a thing as reincarnation, you hope to come back as a proctologist.

- In high school you were voted Most Likely To Get The Death Penalty.

- Sometimes, late at night, you fantasize about going skinny dipping with the Partridge Family.

Mary E. Hirsch

I Ain't Got The Blues, Pinks Or Yellows

Perhaps it is time I make a confession — I am a woman of color. Or a woman of no color. Or perhaps a woman of many colors. I'm not referring to my ethnic or racial background — I'm referring to my home.

A friend told me that my home reminds her of Pee-Wee Herman's Playhouse — only not as tidy. And I take that as a great compliment because not so long ago I lived in a place where everything from the furniture to the planters matched. For me it was hell, a color coordinated hell.

I should have learned my lesson back in the 70's that getting trapped in a color scheme could change a person for life. After an era of psychedelic colors I was caught off guard when I saw everyone's kitchens starting to fill up with appliances and accessories of either avocado green or harvest gold. All around, closing in on me, were these two colors. I felt trapped. The thought of spending my life in an avocado green and harvest gold world scared me. It was worse than my reoccurring nightmare where I'm stuck on a desert island with nothing but Richard Nixon, a Rubik's cube, and an 8-track of Olivia Newton John's greatest hits.

Color evokes all sorts of feelings in each of us. The only thing harvest gold and avocado green evoked in me was a desire to become Amish so I wouldn't be able to see the kitchen once it got dark outside. Avocado green and harvest gold always looked like two colors that were inspired when some designer looked at a dying office plant. But despite my brief, but frightening, excursion into this color abyss of harvest/avocado, I had not learned my lesson.

For many years I tried to pass as a woman with some sort of color scheme . I started out with the best of intentions. After some thought and consideration I chose blue as the color I would use in my home. I had blue curtains on my windows, blue pillows on my chairs, blue sheets on my bed, blue rugs on my floor, and blue water in my toilet. Ironically, I also began to listen to the Blues. But it was all a hopeless charade. No matter how hard I tried to be color coordinated I was just masking the real me. The truth was, although I appeared to be blue on the outside, on the inside I had a tie-dyed heart (not to mention a lava lamp liver).

You see I just love colors — all sorts of colors. For me to limit myself to one or two colors (and perhaps a few socially acceptable complimentary colors) is like trying to wear a pair of size 8 jeans, right after they come out of the dryer, on a day when I'm bloated. It's not an easy fit. In fact, from a purely aerodynamic and physics point of view, it's not a possible fit.

One day, about five years ago, I walked away from a painting that I loved because it didn't go with my decor, which really makes as much sense as not playing a CD because it clashes with your stereo; but that was what I did. I had locked myself into a blue environment. It was just like being a kid again when I was locked in navy blue and vertical-striped clothes in the hopes that no one would notice I was overweight. It was true, colors did evoke a feeling in me — and this time the feeling was entrapment.

MARY E. HIRSCH

So slowly I bought items that didn't match my decor. Trinkets of fire engine red, carrot orange, hot pink, screaming yellow or lime green. I snuck them home and hesitantly displayed them. I think I was afraid the interior decorating police would come along and bust me. But it didn't take long until I had become not just comfortable, but ecstatic with my new found freedom. Today I buy whatever I like (assuming I can afford it or have something left on my credit card limit). It doesn't matter if it clashes with the sofa because the sofa already clashes with the chair which clashes with the lamp which is completely at odds with the bookshelf. But that's okay because none of it clashes with me — a woman of many colors.

Up And At 'Em

One Sunday morning I was lying in bed watching my usual lineup of shows. First there was "CBS Sunday Morning," then "Face The Nation," and then "This Week with Cokie Roberts (and some guy)." Well, during this time I saw a commercial that almost made me sit up in bed — which is not a position I usually take on a Sunday morning. This commercial had former presidential candidate and Senator Bob Dole speaking on behalf of cures for impotence. I'd say you could have knocked me over with a feather, but since I was already lying down that wouldn't work.

At first it appeared he was talking about prostate cancer and encouraging men to get an examination. But soon it became apparent that the main message of the spot was about impotence. I stared in utter shock when Dole spoke about courage and actually compared his struggle with impotence to his fighting in World War II. I was waiting for him to say something like "Before Viagra my little general couldn't salute; my fighter plane had been grounded; you know, my periscope wouldn't go up." It wouldn't have surprised me to see a poster behind him saying "Uncle Sam Wants You To Get It Up."

What came to my drowsy little mind was the irony of this commercial. Not that long ago after former Representative Geraldine Ferraro ran for vice president with Walter Mondale she was in a Pepsi commercial with her daughter. I don't remember the commercial, but I do remember the debate surrounding it. People said she sold out, that she cheapened the office of vice president. Today you would have to set fire to the puppies of disabled

MARY E. HIRSCH

orphans to cheapen a political office, but back then endorsing Pepsi was shocking.

So where is today's furor over Bob Dole, a man who ran for president, who is now pimping for Viagra? What are we saying? Penis good; Pepsi bad? (The only difference between penis and Pepsi is a "p." Coincidence? I think not.)

Perhaps Governor Jesse Ventura has the right idea about politics and marketing. In order to finance campaigns, each candidate should find a product to sell. For instance, if I were running for attorney general (which I would never do because that would require becoming a lawyer and, hey, I'm not that desperate for a job), I could do a commercial something like this: "Hi, I'm Mary Hirsch and I'm running for attorney general. If elected I promise to make crime prevention my first concern, just like Svenson's Home Protection does. Yes, with Svenson's in your own home and me in the Capitol dome, we'll make crime a thing of the past."

Or if I ran for U.S. Representative: "Hello, I'm Mary Hirsch and I want to represent you in the House of Representatives. If elected I plan on cleaning up Washington the same way Handy Dandy Detergent cleans up on wash day. Yes, with me in D.C. and Handy Dandy in your washing machine, our nation will be smelling Yankee Doodle Dandy!"

In fact, if Elizabeth Dole ever runs for president again maybe her campaign slogan can be "Vote For Dole Where 'V' Isn't Just For Victory Anymore!"

Time Is A Terrible Thing To Waste

You never know what you will get in the mail, but there are thousands of direct marketing mailing lists out there, and I have found myself on some of the strangest. I have received the expected pitches from music and book clubs tempting me to join, the L.L. Beanish catalogs tempting me to buy, the religious materials tempting me not to be tempted, and a rather unexpected catalog of explicit adult movies and toys tempting me to — well, you can figure out that one yourself. Most end up in the trash (yes, even the adult movie catalog). But when I received a brochure inviting me to attend a seminar titled "The Organized Woman," I just had to read further.

On the cover was a dignified businesswoman wearing a suit and carrying a briefcase with *The Wall Street Journal* tucked under her arm. My curiosity was piqued: How could I become an organized woman? I searched the brochure for answers: Do I need to prioritize my workload? Do I need to learn to delegate? Do I need to buy a scheduling software program? NO!!! I need to learn "a surprisingly easy way to organize [my] purse and stop wasting time looking for things." Truly, this is correct. A well-organized purse could turn my life around. In fact, I imagine it is messy purses that have held women back for all these years.

For instance, I estimate I could write at least two novels of great social significance in the time I spend trying to find my nail clipper. And, to add insult to injury, I'm sure that by now I could have launched a Fortune 500 company that rivals Microsoft if only I hadn't wasted all that time searching for lip gloss. But worst of all, can I

Mary E. Hirsch

ever forgive myself for frittering away my time hunting for those darn keys when I could have been finding a cure for the common cold? All those years I thought a bigger purse was the answer, but now I know it was a complete lack of organization.

And what else can "The Organized Woman" seminar help me with? Did you know there are "Five surprising things you can accomplish while standing in line, sitting in traffic or waiting for an appointment"? I didn't. What could those five surprising things be? I can only speculate: 1) roll bandages for the Red Cross; 2) do facial isometrics to tighten up my jaw line; 3) memorize Victorian poetry; 4) give birth; and — need I say it — 5) organize my purse.

Until I got this brochure I never really thought that organizational skills differed for men and women. But I guess there are different skills for different genders. Of course, now I wonder what is being offered at "The Organized Man" seminar. Is he learning three easy ways to organize the change in his pants pocket so he doesn't look like he's pleasuring himself? Or perhaps there are five surprising things he could accomplish while standing at the urinal. It boggles the mind.

Of course I'll never know the real answers to these important questions because I cannot attend "The Organized Woman" seminar. I realize this seminar could be the turning point of my career, and it's hard not to sign up when I could learn purse organization and constructive line-standing activities, and the promise to learn "how to ensure...hair stylists and others will get [me] in on time", but I can't find my checkbook to pay for the seminar and I broke a nail looking for my appointment book to see if that date is clear and I think it is being held on the same day I have to stand in line for Julio Iglesias concert tickets. Oh, well—maybe next year when I'm better organized.

**"I use to dress for success but my
jock strap kept riding up on me!"**

MARY E. HIRSCH

"Freud was right! Every payday I have penis envy."

Birth Of A Notion: What Freud Forgot To Tell You

The following is from a paper recently delivered at the annual meeting of TRUE (Theories 'R Us, Etc.) by Dr. Sara Floyd. Dr. Floyd is considered by many to be the mother of modern psychiatry.

* * *

Madam President, members of the executive committee, sisters and fellow seekers of truth and knowledge, I come here tonight to deliver a paper I believe will change the course of the world. It can now be told that the notion of penis envy as the guiding force in women's lives is nothing but a phallicsy that is as flaccid as those who erected its conception. In fact it was simply a sheath for the real psychological phenomenon that exists in our society. I have discovered that 99% of all males suffer from womb envy. (For some unknown reason apparently the other 1% are pro wrestlers.)

This theory first penetrated my research when I was studying male hysteria. Womb envy, I believe, began with the cave dwellers. At one time humans roamed the earth as equals among all animals. Soon, due to a few well-thrown rocks and some good publicity, the cave dwellers began to see themselves as superior beings. As wars broke out between tribes, the male warrior found that after a hard day of hurling rocks he had an instinctive need to retreat into a cave. The comfort, security and warmth it provided caused him to regress back to the time he was safe in his mother's womb. Ever since then man has retreated to safe secure places attempting to find the womb of tranquility.

Mary E. Hirsch

While some may criticize my theory, I have come to view their ill-conceived criticisms as the rantings of irrational men who cannot accept the fact that they are wombless. I will now cite three irrefutable observations of male behavior to substantiate my thesis.

First, men are constantly retreating into small compact spaces in the name of manliness when actually they are searching for their nonexistent wombs:

- A baseball team waits in a dugout, rubbing and polishing their long, hard, sleek, wooden bats while prematurely spewing wads of thick saliva onto the ground;

- Football teams gather in huddles planning their strategy to score by penetrating upright posts with their long, hard, sleek pigskin balls; and

- Soldiers retreat into foxholes and pup tents while their long, hard, sleek, steel bazookas sit defenselessly out in the open waiting for the moment when they can discharge their ammunition.

If these examples aren't enough to convince you of the soundness of my theory consider this: do you think it's only a coincidence that the President of the United States works in an Oval office. Ovalating is the closest man will ever come to ovulating.

These are all vehicles for men to escape from the cold and harsh external environment of the world into warmth and safety, which leads to my second observation: Men hate the fact that their sex organs are hanging out of their body. There are two obvious reasons for these feelings. First, men are exposed and subjected to their environment. While the womb has a constant 98.6° climate, a penis can fry in the Sahara or freeze in the Arctic. Have you ever heard of a womb getting caught in a zipper? The pelvic bone protects the womb from injury but a well-placed kick can, on the other hand, lead a man to contortions reserved for sideshows and people whose laxatives have all of a sudden started working. Actually, a well-placed kick to the groin also seems to disable every man who witnesses the attack. Second, having your genitals hanging outside your body is just plain messy. While growing up little boys watched as price tags or threads hanging from clothes were snipped-off as unsightly. These boys were always tucked securely into bed, never left with one leg hanging out of the covers, dangling aimlessly towards the floor. They saw icicles hanging from the eaves batted away and smashed into little pieces. Is it any wonder why men suffer from womb envy? They have been taught to tuck it in, pick it up, put it away, not to let it hang out. Have you ever noticed the fuss made over an open fly?

It is this idea of messy genitalia which leads to the third and final observation which substantiates my theory. It came from studying the male sex drive. Contrary to popular opinion, the male sex drive is not an act of power or strength, rather sex is an attempt to hide the unsightly penis. This explains the differentiation in the sex drive of men and women. Women, content in the wholeness of their body (a place for everything and everything in its place), feel no urge to rush into intercourse. Men, on the other hand, have this intense urge to conceal their genitalia and thus hurry along to intercourse. Therefore, intercourse is the male's attempt to neaten up the world —

MARY E. HIRSCH

BEAUTIFY THE EARTH:
Plant A Tree; Hide A Penis.

The manifestations of womb envy can cause men to go to great extremes to become like the womb possessors, even if they cannot possess the womb. For instance, some men have taken to washing dishes, sharing their feelings, and going into women's work. (Some have even gone so far as to enter the field of nursing, thus exhibiting their secondary tendency towards mammary envy).

How do we treat such a psychosis? How do we help men and boys see that they can be whole human beings without having wombs? That they can succeed despite their penis?

To begin with we need to provide strong role models of men who have overcome their penis and become successful. Womb envy should be brought into the open where it can be confronted and discussed on television programs with Oprah, Ricki and that woman with the funny red glasses. A study of the topic can become a best seller, such as my new book about to be published entitled **"MAKE WOMB FOR DADDY: Men Who Want It All."** With the proper guidance, support and federal regulations, every person, even those without wombs, can have a chance at a fulfilling life.

Undoubtedly this new discovery will have a backwash. Paranoid, hysterical men will try to re-erect the penis envy theory, engorging the public with its ideas, and thrusting itself on fertile minds. But rest assured, as always, this act of self-manipulation is short lived and will soon leave the public unsatisfied. Thank you for your consideration of my theory.

"Oh for heaven's sakes people -- this shouldn't be so tough"

Mary E. Hirsch

WILL WRITE HAIKU FOR FOOD

How do poets earn a living? I know of very few people who can honestly list "POET" as their occupation when filing their income taxes. This doesn't seem quite fair. After all, aspiring novelists, journalists, etc. can often find jobs that allow them to write -- to express their creativity. While they may not be able to write brochures with complex symbolism or interviews of local celebrities brimming with irony, they are at least writing. But poets usually have to find careers that have nothing to do with poetry.

I think that's because poets and poetry have never been properly marketed. People don't realize how often they could use a poet. Maybe corporations wouldn't need a full time poet, but there should be a temporary agency where people can hire a poet when they find themselves faced with a situation where a poem is needed. And because the public may not be aware of their drastic need for a poet, that need will have to be created by a team of marketing masterminds. After all there was a time when we thought we didn't need foot powder, feminine hygiene sprays or singing fish? With good public relations and creative advertising it won't be long before we will be seeing ads for:

LAUREATE:
THE POET'S TEMPORARY AGENCY

T'was once a poet named Bob,
Who t'was compelled to perform certain jobs,
But his heart t'was in rhyme,
E'er all of the time,
Which setteth him apart from the mob.

All successful businesses occasionally need a sonnet, a jingle, or an epic trilogy, and your business is no different. Whether you own a professional athletic team in need of cheers, have a special client you want to say thank you to but just can't find the right couplet, or sense that your annual reports could bring in new investors with just the right iambic pentameter -- Laureate is for thou!

Our resident faculty of poets are ready to release their muse in order to fill your poetic needs. Here are some reflections from a few of our satisfied patrons:

Our _ _ _ _ing careers were in the _ _ _ _ing toilet until that _ _ _ _ _ing Alexi chick translated some ancient Gregorian chants into rap songs that are climbing the _ _ _ _ing charts.

                                        The Squeeze Boys

Justice was well served when True turned a dull, stale, wrongful death brief into an epic poem. His turn of a phrase was a turn of the tides in favor of our client and helped us obtain a $1.5 million settlement that really putteth the screws to the other side.

                                        J. W. Jones, Esq.

Okay. Like our sports teams, you know, like they were like so good — NOT — until this totally awesome poet Kristoffer, you know, wrote us like some radical new cheers. Now, like, no matter how bogus our team is, you know, *we* still look good and get lots of dates with the really great guys!!!

Jenni, Krissi, Heidi,
Barbi, Debi and Margo
— The West High Pep Squad

Even though we will never acknowledge any dealings with her, if we had hired Noelle (which we didn't) to create a new top secret code book using meter and rhyme (which we don't have) we know she would have done a Yankee Doodle Dandy job. But we didn't do that so ignore what we just said and remember the snow melts slowly in the Arctic.

The Armadillo, CIA

Remember, at Laureate our motto is:

> With a smile —
> SERVICE
>   given!!!!!
> Total sat-is-faction —
>   you get or we ....
>   s
>   i
>   n
>   k
> into despair.

Have a cloudless and congenial day!!!

Of course if this idea does catch on, can you imagine the IRS trying to decide if incense, herbal teas, cat food and Bohemian clothing are deductible?

Vegetarians returning home from the hunt.

MARY E. HIRSCH

**"He's stuck in the 60's but shoots
in the 70's"**

A Shady Friendship

Last week the City of Minneapolis cut down my tree. Well technically, it belonged to the rest of the city because it was on the boulevard, but because I had watched it for more than eight years from my window, I feel the rest of the city can relinquish their ownership and let me refer to it as my tree.

After all, I saw it without its leaves, it saw me without my leaves and that is just about as intimate as two living objects can get without becoming co-dependent, sharing bodily fluids, or ending up on Jerry Springer.

For the past year I had a feeling my tree was dying, but I was in denial. Considering that in high school biology I put on my test that there are two types of trees — deciduous and carnivorous — I hoped that my lack of tree knowledge would prove me wrong about my tree's health. But, much to my amazement (and probably the amazement of the entire faculty of Southwest High), this time I was right. My tree was dying. But the reality of it didn't hit until I arrived home one day to find my tree had the dreaded orange circle painted around it. In Minneapolis when a tree is dead, and has to be cut down, an orange circle is painted around it.

In all the years that Minneapolis has been applying the orange ring of death on local trees, I have never seen the person who does the dirty work. It's as if there is a Grim Limb Reaper who stalks the streets when no one is around and quickly applies an orange stripe to unfortunate trees to mark his timber territory — much to the envy of every dog in the neighborhood.

MARY E. HIRSCH

I have this horrible feeling that some day my health insurance provider will show up at the door with his actuarial tables in one hand and a can of orange paint in the other, and I will be marked as a high risk. Of course if some incredibly well-built lumberjack came along later it might be worth it — but I digress.

It wasn't long after the orange line appeared that I arrived home to find my tree had been given a flat-top. All the small branches were gone, and the limbs had been cut away leaving an object that looked more like a coat rack than a tree. I knew it was only a matter of time before my whole tree would be gone. It was cut down on a Tuesday while I was at home. I started to watch from my window but found myself walking away. The kids at the pre-school across the street turned away too. What I thought would take hours took about 15 minutes. It was there . . . it was gone . . . and all that was left was a stump. Kind of reminded me of my marriage (but once again I digress).

A few days after the removal I called Ben, one of the city's foresters, and asked what happens now that my tree is gone. Will there be a memorial service? Will the sawdust and chips be placed in an urn on some ecologist's mantle? Would the stump be removed or would it remain so my local politicians could stand on it and give speeches?

Ben told me that the stump would be removed and said I could request that a new tree be scheduled for planting next spring. The other day I attempted to count the rings on the stump before it was removed to try to discover just how old my tree had been. Something in me wanted to be able to write one of those "Hard Copy" quips saying that my tree had been here for hundreds of years yet it only took 15 minutes to destroy. But my best estimate is 32 rings, which means I'm older than my tree and, ironically, sometimes on a bad day my hair looks like a bird has nested in it.

Now if I were a poet, or philosopher, or Leo Buscaglia, I might write about how the loss of my tree reflects the circle of life or how we don't appreciate things until they are gone or something else incredibly deep and provocative, but I'm not. And I know losing my little tree is a flea on the rump of an elephant compared to the destruction of millions of trees in the rain forests. But I miss my tree, and tomorrow if I drive by your house and see there is an orange ring on your tree, I want you to know I'm sorry.

MARY E. HIRSCH

Born To Sit

The Cold War may be over, but the scars have not healed for all of its victims — including yours truly. You see, I'm suffering from Cold War Syndrome. Sure, a lot of people remember the Cold War as a time of witch hunts, atomic testing, the race to space and the Cuban missile crisis. I, on the other hand, remember it as a time of personal pain and suffering — yes, it was the time when President John F. Kennedy started the President's Council on Physical Fitness, a diabolical plot to torture the overweight, uncoordinated and lethargic children of America.

Apparently, after viewing tapes of healthy and fit children in Communist countries, Kennedy decided it was time to punish all American children for watching too much television, eating too many Twinkies, and having parents who voted for Nixon. The Red Menace had hit home and invaded our school gymnasium in the form of a test — the President's National Physical Fitness Test.

The first thing they did was weigh you. Being a calorically challenged child the only thing I imagined that could have been worse than being weighed in front of your third grade class was if you were naked at the time and your mother was cleaning your face with spit on a tissue.

The first event you had to do was the 50-yard dash, or in my case the 50-yard saunter. Apparently Communist kids were always running 50 yards and so we had to run 50 yards in order to keep up with them. It made no sense to me why any kid, Communist or Capitalist, should run as fast as she could toward absolutely nothing. There weren't cupcakes, Slinkys or Bobby Darin posters 50 yards away, so why hurry to get there? A real skill would be the 60-second network commercial dash — can you go to the bathroom, get a snack and annoy your brother before the commercial break is over? Now that was the test where I knew I could beat any Russian kid.

Then there was the dreaded rope climb. I remember looking at the rope hanging from the gymnasium ceiling, then looking at my chubby form, and finally looking at my gym teacher and asking "Does the word 'gravity' mean anything to you?" Apparently this guy really expected me to climb to the top. It seems rather criminal to allow a person who is so out of touch with reality to become a teacher. I felt that triumphantly standing on the large knot at the bottom of the rope was enough exercise of me.

And if you haven't suffered enough, here comes the part where you're supposed to do 50 sit-ups? What is it with 50? First you have the 50-yard shuffle, I mean dash, and now you are supposed to do 50 sit-ups. What's so bad about, say, 45 or 46? I managed to do about 15 or 16 sit-ups, at which time my body was so distraught at all of this straining and bending that I began passing gas — loudly. This was not at all welcomed by the poor person holding down my feet, who promptly announced to the entire class, "She let one!" At that moment I lost my sit-up partner and the little bit of dignity I had left after the weigh-in.

There was only one event in which I had a prayer of even coming close to measuring up to the Russians and making President Kennedy proud of me; that was the baseball toss. Now that was a practical skill! You could improve your water balloon lob, fine-tune your snowball

47   MARY E. HIRSCH

aim, and be ready to fling propaganda pamphlets over the Berlin Wall whenever the president needed you. That day when my baseball throw put me in the top 90 percentile I was one of the few, the proud, the American ball tossers. To this day I'm sure Communism fell just because the KGB got wind of my ball-tossing capabilities.

Needless to say I did not get a Presidential Fitness patch, or a certificate, or a chance to go to Washington, D.C. and serve my country by running 50 yards really fast across the White House lawn. But I did get the satisfaction of knowing I did my best and, while everyone else was outside practicing for the tests, I finally got to see what the boys' bathroom looked like. You wouldn't believe what's in there!!!

Honey, I Shrunk The Id

I have a tendency to look for the quick fix, the easy out and the absolute truth in books preferably with large print, few pages, fun covers, and catchy titles. And I'm not the only one. Bookstores and libraries are filled with books that promise the reader better lives. Complexes, psychoses and other life problems are boiled down to a snappy title. Some of the most popular books have featured storybook characters as metaphor for psychological phenomenons. I call them the little golden books of psychology. There is *The Cinderella Complex, The Peter Pan Syndrome, The Snow White Syndrome* and *The Wendy Dilemma*. This approach to self-help is limitless. Some future books you may see are:

The Goldilocks Complex: This is an insightful look at the problems faced by blond women who go from bed to bed in search of love, approval and a hot meal.

The Rapunzel Riddle: The best study of high society women who just can't let their hair down even if it would release them from the prison keeping them from committing to a fulfilling and satisfying relationship.

The Jack & Jill Quandary: Here we examine why women who are successfully climbing the corporate ladder give it all up to follow some clumsy oaf who is headed down hill.

The Old Mother Hubbard Cycle: This book examines the characteristics of spiritually impoverished menopausal women who see their infertility as a barren

Mary E. Hirsch

cupboard and worry that they no longer even have a bone to toss to the old dog they married.

The Three Little Pigs Problem: An in-depth look at the lives of men who are short, stout, and homeless.

The Rumplestilskin Condition: A character study of the relationships between working class women and entrepreneurial men with stupid names and too much gold jewelry.

The Wizard of Oz Bind: This book asks: Why do mid-Western women wear gingham-checked outfits in hopes of getting older men to go on road trips with them?

The Pollyanna Puzzle: This book goes beyond the facts and asks the tough question: What happens when perky cheerleaders won't grow up?

The Three Blind Mice Predicament: No where will you find a more accurate look at why farsighted men fear castration.

The Little Red Riding Hood Mystery: At long last, help for women who flaunt their goodies to attract wolves, who eventually will just eat them up and spit them out.

The Humpty Dumpty Effect: Finally, a serious look at obese men who fall apart at the smallest crisis and then expect those around them to pick-up the pieces.

The Jack and the Beanstalk Crisis: The story of men who climb their way to the top in an attempt to please their mothers.

The Frog Prince Issue: A look at ugly, horny men who hang out at their fancy pad all day waiting for beautiful women to set them free.

The Pinocchio Plight: Perhaps the best study of runaway boys with large noses who allow themselves to be kept as puppets by domineering Italian men.

I'm going to start checking the toy shelves at local stores for the next great movement in psychology — Middle-Aged Mutant Jungian Turtles.

Mary E. Hirsch

A New Look At Old Maids

I'm an Old Maid. That is I'm unmarried, have no children and am over the age of 35. Society considers this odd and refers to me as an Old Maid or, sometimes a spinster. I don't mind being an Old Maid. In fact I am quite content to be an Old Maid. Well almost content.

Society perceives an unmarried man with no children (as far as he knows — winkie, winkie) over the age of 35 not as an oddity, but as a walking cult figure. His cronies see him as a deity to manhood — free to have a new woman every night fawning over him, laughing at his jokes, cooking his favorite dishes -- all in a pointless attempt to drag the poor son-of-a-gun to the altar. On the other hand, Old Maids are seen as a cross between Carrie Nation, Mother Teresa and Aunt Bea who spend their time crocheting, baking, and dwelling on their fruitless wombs. They have high buns on their heads, sagging buns on their bodies and social lives that are as exciting as the doilies on their tables.

This myth is perpetuated by the card game Old Maid which depicts Old Maids as women who are involved in hobbies and jobs that are as dainty and frail as the Old Maids themselves. These deprived, barren and pitiful women include such role models as the bespectacled Lily Librarian, the hefty and hearty Norma Nurse, the eccentric Biddie Birdwatcher and, of course, the spry Penelope Piano Teacher. You'd think the person left with the Old Maid card would be the winner.

In an attempt to improve the image of my fellow Old Maids, I created a children's manuscript called "A New Look At Old Maids." It includes folklore and myths around

"Old Maids" and profiles of various women from archaeologists to botanists to doctors to scientists — women who just happen to have never married, had no children, and somehow found more to do with their time than read the personals. In response to my book proposal, an editor wrote:

> "[We] seek to present strong and accomplished women as role models for young readers, but we examine the lives of the women in the context of their areas of expertise. Many of the women featured in [our] series of collective biographies were unmarried, and this fact of their lives is discussed when relevant A book on women as 'old maids,' however, is not appropriate for the series

Perhaps this makes sense, until you discover that this same publisher has a book entitled "America's Most Influential First Ladies." I never knew that marrying well is considered an "area of expertise," but it must be. After all, the catalog at my local library features more than 100 books under the subject of United States Presidents — Wives and not even a listing for United States Presidents — Old Maid Sisters. I suppose I could work on a proposal for a new book that would broaden the scope of marrying well as an area of expertise. One idea that comes to mind is America's Most Influential Wives of Professional Athletes.

Well enough of this fiddle-faddle. I have a busy day ahead of me. There is bread to be baked, roses to be pruned, sachets to be replaced, socks to be darned, Sunday School lessons to be planned and today is my cat Puffball's birthday. But first things first; where did I put this month's copy of *Old Maids Illustrated*? It's the swimsuit issue and I want to check out this year's line of bloomers.

MARY E. HIRSCH

**"Miss America is a scholarship pageant . . .
and I'm a stealth bomber!"**

THE SECRET OF NUCLEAR ATOMICWARE

One of the major stories in 1995 was the 50th anniversary of the atomic bomb. It was commemorated, commentated, debated and denounced with news specials, ceremonies, feature articles, magazine retrospects, speeches, etc. Undoubtedly, the debut of the atomic bomb changed the world. But, did you know that 1995 was the 50th anniversary of another important moment in world history — the debut of Tupperware.

At the same time the government was launching bombs in Los Alamos, New Mexico, Earl D. Tupper was launching bowls in Farnumsville, Massachusetts. Can any of us who have lived through the Warren Commission, Watergate, Iran Contra and Milli Vanilli be expected to believe it is merely a coincidence that the atomic bomb and Tupperware were "introduced" at the same time? That there isn't any government involvement or, dare I say, conspiracy associated with this "coincidence"? That Oliver Stone's next movie won't be called "Atomicware"?

While the actual link between the two inventions may not be obvious at first, a little in-depth research, hypothesizing and paranoia makes it obvious that there is more to atomic weapons and Tupperware than bombing and burping. Does the government think we are going believe and accept that the following "coincidences" are simply nuke flukes:

• You can clear a room just as quickly by announcing you're having a Tupperware party as you can by announcing you're carrying an atomic weapon.

- Old atomic waste is as hard to dispose of as old Tupperware.

- You can't put either one in the dishwasher or microwave without risking some type of meltdown or destruction.

- You push a button to launch an atomic weapon and seal the fate of the world; you push a button to seal a Tupperware bowl.

- A Tupperware party can lead to the total destruction of an evening; an atomic bomb can lead to the total destruction of all evenings.

- **SALT**: **S**trategic **A**rms **L**imitation **T**reaty
  SALT: **S**ell **A** **L**otta **T**upperware

- Atomic weapons supposedly keep the peace; you can keep a piece of pie in Tupperware.

- Tupperware is made of "Poly-T"; nuclear weapons are made by Poli-Tics.

- You can't hug a child with nuclear arms; you can't hug a child with your arms full of Tupperware.

- Truman dropped the bomb; true men drop out of sight during a Tupperware party.

- You use Tupperware to pack a lunch; you use atomic weapons to pack a punch.

- Sil-o; Jell-o. Think about it!

• Governments negotiate a freeze of nuclear weapons; Tupperware is used in a freezer.

• Tupperware is sold at home parties; atomic weapons are sold at political parties.

• Atomic weapons are kept in containers with tight lids; Tupperware makes containers with tight lids

• Tupperware makes a great housewarming gift; atomic weapons will make a house warm — very, very warm.

• If not used properly, both Tupperware and atomic weapons can leak.

• The atom was split to create the atomic bomb; friends split when you announce you're having a Tupperware party.

• Atomic bombs are deterrents to war; Tupperware is a deterrent to mold.

• Atomic bombs are *nuclear* weapons; Tupperware sells *new clear* containers.

• You can never have too much Tupperware; apparently you can never have too many atomic weapons.

• Tupperware and atomic bombs are the two most interesting things you will find in North Dakota.

While it is obvious that atomic weapons and Tupperware have much in common, the exact significance of these similarities is not yet clear. Perhaps the correlation

MARY E. HIRSCH

between Tupperware and atomic weapons has something to do with CIA agents cleverly disguised as Tupperware ladies used to infiltrate suburban homemaker spy rings. However, until enough evidence to prove these theories can be gathered, take care the next time you "burp" your Tupperware. It could be the belch that is heard around the world.

We Shall Overcome...Then We Shall Upholster

When I read the newspaper, I always keep a scissors nearby. It comes in handy if I find an article I want to keep, maybe a coupon for 50 cents off on something chocolate, or Dan Quayle is elected president and I want to take my life.

This passion for cutting out articles that catch my eye has resulted in many great conversations, some good humor essays and a lot of boxes full of a lot of articles that seem to take up a lot of space. The other day I came across an article that I re-read and was struck by a moment of enlightenment — one of those moments that makes me stop and think and say "What the heck?"

Do you ever wonder if the struggles of the women's movement have been worth it? Has anything really been accomplished? Are we any better off today than we were 30 or 40 years ago? If you've ever found yourself asking such questions, an article I saved may help you with your struggle because it certainly cleared things up for me.

Many years ago, the *Minneapolis Star Tribune* had a story in its Sunday edition titled "Ornate Beds Add to Romantic Bedroom Look." In this article Lynn Hollyn, a home furnishings product designer, said "the success of the women's movement is in part responsible for today's romantic [bedroom] look. As we embark on the 1990s we are comfortable in expressing our femininity, which wasn't always the case earlier." That explains a lot to me.

For years I thought the women's movement was about equal rights, better working conditions, more opportunity for women, children's rights, pay equity, etc.

Mary E. Hirsch

But, I was wrong. The women's movement is about making the world safe for dust ruffles. But do I have a dust ruffle? NO!!! I have dust, and I think there are some Ruffles potato chips ground into the carpet, but I don't think that's the dust ruffle Ms. Hollyn had in mind. I should be flogged with a valance (preferably a soft rose or peach-tone valance because "these are colors that make a woman look her best and ... suggest a romantic environment").

When I think that the women's movement could be responsible for this great accomplishment, and hundreds more that I don't even know about, I can't help but wonder why there is all this fuss about an Equal Rights Amendment? After all, we've got our dust ruffles. What more could we want?

Halfway To Dead

I'm about to turn 45. My knees are creaking, my back aches, I have to get up at least once at night to tinkle, and I find myself paying attention to retirement commercials. This really pisses me off. I remember when I turned 25 and the big joke was "You're half way to 50!" Well at 45 you rarely hear anyone say "You're half way to 90" because it's kind of like saying you're half way to dead.

I'm sure it's not a big surprise to hear me say that I don't intend to grow old gracefully — virtually everybody says it in one way or another. But in the past few weeks I have been wondering exactly what does the idea of staying young mean to me?

Many times when people, especially women, say they're going to fight aging, what they're referring to is how they look. This was brought home to me in a recent Oprah show (yes, I watch Oprah). Joan Rivers was on the show and she was talking about a book she just wrote on fighting the aging process. The show focused on how you look and the goal was not so much to look younger than you are, but to look your best where you are now. There were some astonishing make-overs and lots of talk about hair, make-up and clothing and, I admit, I paid closer attention than I would have five or ten years ago. (I also had the volume up a little louder than I would have five or ten years ago and was peering at the picture over my reading glasses.)

What upset me was the comment about plastic surgery. First, Rivers suggested that every women should have a face lift. But it was how she said it that really fried my bacon. When they spoke of the expense for such a procedure and that the average woman couldn't afford it, Rivers said something to the effect of I'd rather see a beautiful woman get out of an old run down car than an old run down woman get out of a beautiful car, suggesting that if you can afford a new car, you can afford a face lift. What bothers me is not just that the statement was cold, heartless, harsh, cruel and stupid; but that it's stayed with me. Now I look in the mirror and see the lines I never really noticed before. In fact I've been forced to thoroughly clean my mirror just so I can be sure it's a line I'm seeing and not just a dirt streak. And let me tell you, anything that upsets me enough to force me to clean is a major event in my life.

I have spent my entire life fighting the "look" factor and I have a feeling that the fight isn't going to end when I turn 45. I have gray hair, wrinkles and lines, and if much more of my body heads south I'll be able to declare myself a resident of Iowa. But even if I never change any of these physical features, I don't intend to grow old gracefully with or without a face lift. Anyone for a game of Candyland?

HEBONICS — THE LANGUAGE OF MAN

There's been a debate in America about our culture and its language—well actually languages. Ebonics was at the center stage and whether or not it should be recognized as a second language. I personally don't know what all the fuss is about — every culture and group has a language of its own. For example, all my life I have had to struggle to understand Hebonics — the true language of man.

Some Hebonics have become part of our culture and are easy to recognize. For example in Hebonics "a cold one" means beer; "seven course dinner" means a six-pack and a hot dog; and "chick movie" means any film where a feeling is expressed, nothing blows up, and not enough breasts are shown to make it worth watching.

Like many languages, Hebonics has feminine and masculine phrases for the same word or action. For instance, the feminine phrase for vacuuming, dusting, washing, sweeping, and doing other things in a house that keeps it clean is "housekeeping." The masculine phrase for the same event is "helping around the house." And the reverse is true too — the masculine phrase for people who fight for their country in combat is "soldier," the feminine phrase is "helping around the war."

An example of Hebonics can be found in how the word "babysitting" is redefined. In traditional English, "babysitting" means someone who is taking care of other people's children either for pay or as a favor. In Hebonics, "babysitting" means, "My wife isn't home and I'm stuck with the kids."

MARY E. HIRSCH

Hebonics was a common part of recent presidential elections. Normally a person who enjoys watching a sport is a fan; but if that person happens to be a woman and the athlete she is watching happens to be her child she is no longer a "fan," she becomes a "soccer mom." Not only does that mean she is more likely to vote for a specific candidate, but she is also the person who is required to bring treats for the team.

Objects are defined Hebonically. For example, "library" has traditionally meant a place where people go to read and study; in Hebonics it means "bathroom." The "family car" is not a car shared by the family, it is the car that Mom drives — the one with the candy wrappers, juice boxes and a CD player that doesn't work because there are melted Gummy Bears inside.

When it comes to word games you can count on Hebonics as one of the players. Here is a classic Hebonics acronym. Everyone has heard a guy say, "This weekend I'm gonna get me 'some.'" The Hebonically impaired believe "some" means sex. Ha! This is not true. "Do It" means sex. In the world of Hebonics "some" is an acronym for "**S**ofa, **O**ld **M**ilwaukee and **E**SPN."

There are some nonverbal Hebonic communications. For example, flagellating is his way of saying "I feel comfortable with you," and belching really means "Hey, that was a great dinner!" Of course, waving an index finger at anyone is a cross-gender (Hebonics/Shebonics) way of saying "pardon me, but I beg to differ."

And if you should ever find yourself at a sports bar watch out, if you stay there too long you could catch the Hebonic Plague.

Geri saw menopause not as a problem but as an opportunity.

Mary E. Hirsch

GRAMPS

Like most urban cities, the sidewalks, bus shelters, billboards, store fronts, etc. of my city have been spray painted with the symbols of various gangs. These artistic endeavors are apparently left by gang members in an effort to tell the world they've been there -- much like dog droppings let the world know Rover has been there.

After seeing these masterpieces for a long time I thought I had become oblivious to the doodles and scribbles. They blended in with the markings left by street maintenance and utility workers. But the other day a cryptic message scrawled on a semaphore control box caught my eye:

G R A M P S

Just the name itself sent a chill through my spine. I decided to investigate this new gang, to see what sinister purpose they had to their existence. What I discovered may make you double lock your door, hide under your bed, and join the NRA.

GRAMPS consists of an underground group of men with dentures in their mouths, hair in their combs, and change in their pockets. These are men who will stop at nothing to force innocent children into baseball stadiums, amusement parks, fast food restaurants and video arcades. They are often seen bouncing children senselessly on their knees while singing nonsensical tunes and tickling exposed bellies and ribs.

Many are fooled into believing members of GRAMPS are easy to recognize by mismatched outfits, shuffling feet or slow moving vehicles, and that they are harmless -- but this is not true. GRAMPS are in your neighborhood. You'll find them lurking in barber shops, on golf courses, in movie theaters and banks. They try to blend in with a crowd to take people off guard, but you can usually single them out by their twinkling eyes, quick smiles, strong gaits and guttural noises (often called laughter).

And, if this news isn't bad enough, you should meet their chicks, their main squeezes, their old ladies. You should meet the GRAMS.

These gang members can often be distinguished by gray hair, a wrinkle or two on their face, a blue vein here and there on their legs, a purse filled with candies, and a heart filled with love. Like their old men, GRAMS are ruthless in their efforts to get at your children. They lure them with warm hugs, wet kisses, open ears and a cookie or two. At first they give these cookies and attention free of charge — to get the kids hooked — then they start to make them pay for their pleasures. GRAMS demand homemade art to hang on kitchen walls, photographs of messy faces, and unending stories of what they did today.

PARENTS BEWARE!!!!! These men and women are dangerous. Children who spend time with GRAMPS and GRAMS often develop self-worth, love of life, sense of fun and respect for others. Impressionable youth tend to bond with members of these gangs and strive to be like these new role models.

If you want to stop your children from falling into their clutches, keep them away from our senior citizens whenever possible and if they should fall into the hugs of the old tell them to just say NEW!

MARY E. HIRSCH

**"You're right mother, it's just an
excuse not to take you to the casino."**

Mom's The Word

When Congresswoman Patricia Schroeder was asked how she could be both a politician and a mother, she replied, "Because I have a brain and a uterus." On the second Sunday in May we celebrate Mother's Day — a day that historically has tended to salute only one of the organs Schroeder mentioned.

Mother's Day evokes all sorts of emotions in people. Generally, attitudes fall somewhere between the cynical "Bah Mumbug" stance, which holds the position that Mother's Day is perpetuated by retailers as a way to line their pockets, and the "Apple Pious" belief that motherhood is a sacred calling placing mothers right up there with doctors, popes, honest politicians, and switch-hitters batting over 300.

It is in this abyss between emotions that most of us decide just how to celebrate Mother's Day. Do we ignore it? Do we give it a passing mention with a token gift? Do we create a spectacle of love worthy of a mini-series starring Melissa Gilbert?

If we decide to give a gift, the process of choosing the gift is not terribly difficult because mothers love anything you give them — even the mother who every year says "Don't buy me anything; Save your money; I have everything I could ever want." Flowers and candy are traditional choices, especially for people who need to send their gifts across the country. Clothing, perfume, photographs, dining out, knickknacks, are also common choices. But retailers will try to persuade you that their product is an excellent choice, so you will need to use common sense. Think twice before wrapping up that

Mary E. Hirsch

power drill, gerbil, Meatloaf's "Bat Out Of Hell" CD, steam iron or Monistat 7 gift set. And even if you do find choosing a gift to be fairly easy, you will soon discover that choosing a Mother's Day card is hell.

A visit to local card shops makes a person wonder if it is indeed Mother's Day or XX-Chromosome Day. As soon as you arrive, not only do you feel pressured to find the card that says just the right thing for your mom, but to buy a card for every female you know. There are cards for Mothers, Stepmothers, New Mothers, Mothers-To-Be, Mothers-in-Law, Grandmothers, Great Grandmothers, Aunts, Great Aunts, Sisters, Sisters-in-Law, Daughters, People Who Are Like Daughters, Godmothers, Goddaughters, Nieces, Cousins, Mothers of Dear Friends, People Who Have Been Like a Mother To Me, and Special Friends. There didn't seem to be any cards for women who had unprotected sex in the last 30 days, but that's probably an oversight on the part of the card companies that will be rectified soon. There are "group" cards saying "To Mom From All Of Us" which is the same as saying all your kids are cheap. There are "I Remember" theme cards that recall Mom's purse, Grandma's house and wash day. None of them recall the time your mother took out all your baby pictures and showed them to your date. There is a card that says "I Wish I Could Take You To The Bahamas" but not an "I Wish I Could Take You To Des Moines" card. At one store there was even a Mother's Day card for fathers, thanking the recipient for all of his "fatherly mothering." Does that mean while changing your diaper he discussed how the designated hitter rule has ruined baseball or when you hurt yourself he told you the story of General Patton?

And if a Mother's Day card for fathers wasn't bad enough, you can send cards from dogs (animals — not unattractive children) or cats. Imagine the joy of receiving a card claiming that no matter how many people I sniff, I could never find a better crotch than yours.

The most complex card (Oedipus complex, that is) is the Mother's Day card from a husband to his wife. These aren't cards that say thanks for being such a great mom and putting up with our kids; these are cards right out of cable's pay-per-view station. They claim "motherhood is sexy," are written to "my wife, my lover, my friend," and talk about "our souls coming together" and "feeling your skin whispering to mine — love." Perhaps the underlying meaning of these cards is "I Remember a Sex Life."

Of course, no matter how hard card companies try — and they do try hard — there are some categories that fall through the cracks. For instance, there are no cards from nursing babies to moms ("Thanks for the mammaries") or for a friend's sister's mother-in-law's doctor ("I know you don't know who the hell I am but because you are a woman I feel obliged to send you a Mother's Day card"), or for an aunt doing five to ten for armed robbery ("Auntie, Although you are in the big house my love for you knows no bars"). Of course, thanks to create-your-own card machines and software, these gaps can be filled. Whether you're a compulsive eater ("Mom, you are the creme filling in the Twinkie of life") or an attorney ("If I had been given the option to choose a maternal parental unit, of all the maternal parental units in the known biosphere, you are heretofore my foremost choice") or the fitness fanatic ("When it comes to moms, you are the maximum working heart rate in the workout of life"), there is the potential for just the right card.

Finally, no matter if you do or don't choose to celebrate Mother's Day, there's one thing you should remember: God spelled backwards is Dog, but Mom spelled backwards is still Mom. Think about it.

On Writing Bad Poetry

I don't get poetry, not really. I do understand some of it, like a bit of it, and am in awe of a few poems but, in general, I don't get it. Unfortunately, my college advisor insisted I enroll in a class on poetry writing in order to "round out" my education. So one day, faced with a class deadline, I decided to write some poetry.

To be a poet, I figured you must first be centered so I moved to the center of my bed where I crossed my legs and closed my eyes. The phone rang. It was my mother.

"What's new?" she sounded hopeful, as she always did at the start of our conversations.

"I'm trying to be a poet," I announced.

"Oh," she said. I knew she was hoping for something a little more prestigious to brag about to her friends. Something like a rich husband, a boyfriend who was employed, a rich husband, a potential boyfriend who was employed or a rich husband. Actually I knew she'd be happy just to hear that the holes in my earlobes had grown shut so I couldn't wear those long, dangling, harlot earrings she always saw me in. "I know a poem," she continued -- I cringed.

"Roses are red, Violets are purple, You're as sweet, As maple surple."

I gave my nervous laugh, the same laugh I have when I'm in the chair at the dentist's office. "Well that's not quite what I need but thanks."

After a brief discussion about my obvious lack of concern with her obvious over abundance of concern with the way I'm running my life, we hung up.

I then unplugged my phone because poetic geniuses should not be disturbed (except in psychological ways) and returned to my centering position -- waiting for waves of inspiration on what to write a poem about to wash over my soul.

My first thought was about what I was going to have for dinner that night. I tried to wipe this thought from my mind because it didn't strike me as inspiring and besides it would involve eating the flesh of another living thing (with a lot of A-1 sauce) and I wasn't sure poets were allowed to do that.

I then turned my thoughts to nature; an ever inspiring theme for poetry. An image of a rainbow came to my mind so I decided to write about rainbows. I scrambled from my Sealy Posturepedic think-tank to my desk and wrote:

RAINBOWS
at the top of the page.

Rainbows come after the rain

I began. I was inspired.

Like worms crawling out onto sidewalks

was the next line. This was good. I'd thought about rainbows and worms. I linked them into a metaphysical relationship.

But I don't mind Rainbows,
cause I don't have to worry
about stepping on them and
squishing them to death.

It seemed a bit long for a poem stanza. Poets, as I recalled,
left out a lot of grammar like modifiers and verbs, so I
started again, taking it from the top:

RAINBOWS
Rainbows — after the rain
Appear like worms upon sidewalks

Using "—" let me drop all kinds of words and "upon"
seemed an excellent touch.

Rainbows — I don't mind
I can't squish them under my feet.

Something was wrong. "Rainbows—I don't mind." What
real poet would "mind" a rainbow? Would Robert Frost
"mind" two roads in a woods? Rainbows are those
moments poets long for.

Rainbows — I welcome thee
Unlike worms under my feet

"Thee" and "feet" kind of rhymed — I just got lucky on
that one.

Taunting me to play God
And chose their fate

Oh, that was **really** good. It had a twinge of co-dependent symbolism in it so I might be able to read it at my support group.

Rainbows thee crown my head with glory

Very spiritual; but too many words.

Rainbows — crowning my head with glory
I choose thee over worms.

This is pretty good.

RAINBOWS
Rainbows — after the rain
Appear like worms upon sidewalks
Rainbows — I welcome thee
Unlike worms under my feet
Taunting me to play God
and chose their fate
Rainbows — crowning my head with glory
I choose thee over worms.

That only took about ten minutes. I decided to do another. Returning to my centering position I waited for inspiration. My nose started to itch. I reached to scratch it but stopped. I was acutely aware that this may be a message from my poetic muse. I returned to my desk, which by then I had redesignated as my Virginia Woolf Memorial Writing Space.

MY SOUL ITCHES

I couldn't believe how the words just flowed from my Bic.

My soul itches
Longing for God to scratch it

This was deep.

But it goes unsatisfied

This was incredible.

Like the unpicked nose.

This was stupid.

Now my entire body itched along with my soul. My ears crackled as I burped up the taste of sausage pizza from lunch. None of these bodily functions seemed to pull on my soul anymore. I had lost the moment — I was a carpe diem failure.

I noticed my one and only plant in the corner looked impotently withered, and I resolved to water it later — when I got back from the video store. The new Harrison Ford movie was in. I glanced at my writing space as I walked towards the door.

Perhaps I'm not a poet and I know it.

MARY E. HIRSCH

Ovaries With An Attitude!

ATTITUDE PROBLEM

Every time I think the world couldn't get any
stranger I find another example of the coming apocalypse.
For instance, did you know that you can now buy diapers
with attitudes? It's true. I saw it at Target. Apparently
what gives these diapers an attitude is the funky design on
them. What also gives them an attitude is the added cost
for the funky design. The more attitude you want in a
product, the more money you'll have to pay.

Once the domain of teachers, drill sergeants and
mothers (three careers that are often interchangeable),
"Attitude" has become a popular buzzword with
advertisers, media, corporations and motivational speakers.
The only other word that comes close to excessive usage in
the corporate world is "Team." Every time I am referred to
as a team member I have an urge to chew some tobacco,
spit on the ground, and scratch my privates. At least the
word "team" is fairly well defined. You know you are a
member of a group that is suppose to work together — at
least when the boss is around.

But the word "attitude" often stands on its own —
an unmodified noun (or a dangling participle or something
like that which you grammar freaks can figure out and then
write a letter to me chastising my language skills). You
aren't told what kind of attitude a car or soft drink or diaper
has. Is it positive, negative, good, bad, wrong or right?
Who knows — it just has an attitude.

What I think people try to convey with the use of
"attitude" is that a product has some kind of edge over
other products. There is something a little special about it
because it's not like all the other products it is competing

MARY E. HIRSCH

with — it is a rebel of sorts. And, the idea is, if you choose a product with an attitude you too are a bit of a rebel. It's the same mentality that tells us we will play basketball better if we wear the shoes Michael Jordon wears, will be rich if we invest where Jackie Collins invests, or will look like Kim Alexis if we cure our yeast infection with her favorite product. Somehow I have a feeling I could sit in a vat of Monistat cream for 15 years and never even come close to looking like Kim Alexis. So why do we have such a problem when people as well as products have "attitudes."

I can't begin to tell you how many times I've been told I have an attitude problem because I don't conform to a rule or I question what I'm being told or feel that the posted speed limit is simply a suggestion with no binding contract. Is there an attitude monitor somewhere that I'm not aware of? The employee who gives 150% is said to have a good attitude. Of course, that person's family who is getting minus 50% may say he or she has a bad attitude. If you bring up a problem or conflict in a discussion you have a negative attitude as opposed to the person who agrees with everything suggested who is said to have a good attitude. I have found the "good attitude" person usually doesn't know what's going on but will agree to anything as long as it means the meeting is ending and they can get something to eat.

People should have to define what type of attitude they are referring to before giving a person or thing such an assignment. A sports car has a powerful attitude, a soft drink has a rebellious attitude, and the diaper, well I guess it must have a piss-poor attitude.

VIVA LA VIAGRA

On a mild March morning I picked up my Saturday issue of the Minneapolis *Star Tribune* and was greeted with the headline "First pill to treat impotence approved." The same news had been featured on Friday night's local and national news. Being a warm-blooded American female, I'm all for erections, but I'm just not sure this is front page news. I kept waiting for a news promo with a local anchor saying "Old men getting hard-ons. Film at 10:00," but it didn't happen.

That Saturday morning you could almost hear the crackling of skin as smiles came to the faces of men when they read the news about Viagra -- faces that rarely smiled when reading the paper. According to the article, "Studies estimate that 40 percent of 40-year-olds experience mild to severe impotence, as do about 70 percent of 70-year-olds." I just knew there would be some towel-snapping fun in men's locker rooms all across the country as this news was spread.

And glee was also being felt by the stockholders of Pfizer (the manufacturer of Viagra) and in pharmacies when a New York pharmaceutical analyst predicted sales of $300 million for this year alone. Now considering that each tablet will be about $7, that means over 42,850,000 will be sold each year. And this is not a daily pill, this is a pill that needs to be taken about one hour before the man wants to have sex. That means that 42,850,000 times in the next year some guy will turn to his significant other and say "Come on honey. If we don't have sex we'll just be throwing away $7.00."

MARY E. HIRSCH

What interests me most is seeing whether or not the insurance companies decide to cover Viagra for any man. There are many men who indeed suffer from impotence because of spinal injuries, diabetes, prostate surgery and other definable causes, and it would only seem logical that Viagra would be a covered expense for them, as would any other treatment for impotence. But the fact that 70% of all 70 year old men suffer from impotence seems significant in itself. Is impotence a disease or a natural occurrence of the aging process? From what I know, 70% of all 70 year old women suffer from sagging breasts but I don't think Blue Cross will be paying for Wonder Bras in the near future.

Before I'm accused of being a man-hating, castrating, woman, I know impotence can cause terrible psychological problems due to a loss of self-esteem as well as contribute to the breakdown of many relationships. I think Viagra, and any other impotence treatments, should be covered by insurance companies. There are a few men I know that I would personally be willing to pay for their prescription, if they should ever need one. What bothers me, however, is that more than likely there will be no resistance from insurance companies to this new prescription and, in fact, each prescription will probably come with a sample of Brute cologne, a box of Trojans, and the *Sports Illustrated* swimsuit issue.

Yet, it was not so long ago that women had to fight with their insurance company to have breast reconstruction after losing one or both breasts to cancer. And many still have to fight today. Breast reconstruction was, and often still is, considered frivolous and totally cosmetic. Even though there is evidence that the loss of a breast or both breasts could cause terrible psychological problems due to a loss of self-esteem as well as contribute to the breakdown of many relationships. I have a feeling if health insurance board rooms were not overflowing with testosterone, breast reconstruction would have never been an issue.

This breakthrough, and the subsequent heralding of the good news, simply illustrates the difference between the way women and men are treated by the medical community. Perhaps I'm a little paranoid (at least that's the diagnosis of the people who are following me) but does anyone else find it suspicious that the two most recent breakthroughs in medicine have been in the areas of hair replacement and impotence? Can a cure for ear hair be far behind?

**"Look! It's God's Gift To
Pollination!"**

SWF Seeks Translator With Great Abs

What's black and white and dread all over? A newspaper with a Get Acquainted/Personals section to help all of us lonely singles find that special someone. These sections are the source of laughs, lust, love and an occasional movie about a crazed killer. These sections also have a language of their own — Personalese.

At first its easy. You have M or F for gender, S or D for marital status. But then it gets complicated. WW is for widowed so it isn't confused with W which is for white. B is for black, NA for Native American, H for Hispanic and A for Asian. Personally I don't care if you are a BAHNAW, but if you believe Jim Carrey is a comic genius, live with your mother, or think beer is the perfect breakfast, I don't want anything to do with you.

Once you get beyond sex and race Personalese becomes more elaborate. There is N/S for non-smoker, N/D for non-drinker, P for professional (this means you have a business card, a cell phone, and like to "do lunch") and G for gay. Without a G, it is assumed you are an S, unless you are a BI. Recently I noticed the addition of ISO which is someone "In search of" (not necessarily Leonard Nimoy) and LTR which is "long term relationship." So you could be an ISOLTR which looks to me like speedwriting for "isolator" and not the kind of person you want to get involved with unless you have a secret desire to spend the rest of your life in a log cabin churning butter and bearing young 'uns.

If Personalese is going to include ISO, LTR, etc. there are some other abbreviations that should be added to

Mary E. Hirsch

the list. How about DLAS (drinks like a sailor), SLAC (smokes like a chimney), BLDS (breath like dirty socks), and DULL (as interesting as the last issue of Popular Crocheting)? If we have J for Jewish and C for Christian there should be N for new ager, H for heathen, ? for agnostic, and 2 for the folks who show up at church on Christmas Eve and Easter. Other lifestyle abbreviations could include NM for vegetarians, JK for jocks, COD for co-dependent and 12S for any one in treatment for any thing. Standard abbreviations could also be used. Are you an ESQ, an MD, a DDS, a CPA, a CEO, or an SOB (which in some cases is redundant)?

A real time saver would be an MMLC. It would represent a male in a mid-life crisis who is looking for a blonde, not older than 21, who never goes out when "Friends" is on and has a closet full of spandex.

But I don't need the Personals to find a guy. I have a great track record finding an AH on my own.

Ode To A Lost Friend

I recently experienced the loss of a close friend — a friend who has seen me through good times and bad, sickness and health, richer and (mostly) poorer, frozen and thawed — a friend who was always there when needed, always ready to help me out.

I mourn the death of my microwave.

I had this miracle of modern-day technology for more than 10 years and now it's just another trinket on the scrap pile of life. In memory of my microwave I'd like to share this open letter.

Dear Microwave:

I'll never forget the day we first met. It was my birthday and I told my family that the only thing I wanted was you, and there you were. You looked so nice and new in your cardboard box surrounded by Styrofoam peanuts, instructions and promise — the promise that I would again fix a hot meal at home. I could hardly wait to get you back to my place.

Sure at first we were a little nervous, getting to know each other, but those first few months were magnificent as we tried one new thing after another — noodles, pizza, Hot Pockets, soups, popcorn — anything we wanted to try. We were young and giddy with excitement at our new relationship.

I know at times I was hard to live with. There were those moment when I was impatient with you, wondering

Mary E. Hirsch

why it was taking so long for a potato to bake or popcorn to pop.

Sometimes I abused you by opening and shutting your door checking to see if my food was done, treating you as if you weren't capable of living up to your full potential. I never meant to make you feel inferior; it was only my own personal hunger that made me forget how capable you were. If only you were still here I would learn how to give you my food and walk away knowing it was in good hands.

I often took you for granted. I didn't wash your turntable as often as I should. Sometimes I would be in such a hurry to meet my own needs I would forget to use some sort of protection and food would splatter all over you. That was inconsiderate and I can only hope that wherever you are now you can find it in your hardware to forgive me.

But there were plenty of good times. Remember the first time I cooked a hot dog, didn't pierce it and BOOM it blew up? Boy, did we laugh over that one. Or the time I actually made popcorn without burning it. I don't think I slept a wink that night.

I will miss your gentle hum as you cooked my food, the glow that came from your window as you went about your work, and the sound of your "DING" when you were ready for me.

Yes, I know you would want me to go on — on to find another microwave to meet my needs — I know that is what you would want because you were always so giving.

And sure, some day, maybe I will replace you — but you were my first and nobody ever forgets their first.

In conclusion I would like to share a poem I wrote about you. I call it "From Micro to My-cro"

There is one less ding in my kitchen,
One less warm meal on my tray,
One less electrical wonder,
Since you've gone away.

You started out as my Micro,
Just another kitchen thing,
You soon became my My-cro,
And the Yang to my Ying.

Now we are parted forever,
When I think of you I cry,
You can never be replaced,
Except by a special at Best Buy.

Mary E. Hirsch

Holiday Madness

Public schools and the celebration of holidays is a source of continual debate. First it was Christmas. That can't be celebrated in public schools because it is a Christian holiday (although I've heard rumors that Santa Claus is actually a Buddhist priest the rest of the year). Then it was Easter because it is also a Christian holiday (and even I have to admit the Easter Bunny looks like a Presbyterian to me). Last year a friend of mine told me that his son's school was no longer going to be allowed to celebrate Valentine's Day because it could be considered sexual harassment so instead they had Special Friend Day. This is much better — some poor kid who use to just think no one loved him now will discover that no one thinks he's a special friend.

But the worst travesty of all is the banning of Halloween because, according to some people with more time on their hands than brains in their heads, it is a Satanic holiday. Halloween was, and still should be, the great kid holiday. A chance to use your imagination, dress up in a fun costume, be a little frightened, and best of all, get free candy.

So what can be celebrated? Not much of anything. In fact, I went through a book of holidays and discovered numerous other occasions that we must protect our children from.

Columbus Day — This is a sexist and bias holiday because it celebrates the fact that men are always getting lost and refuse to ask for directions.

Children's Book Day — Far too many trees are being cut down in the rain forests to print books. This day is really celebrating an ecological disaster.

National Smile Week — This discriminates against the grouchy and the grumpy as well as puts pressure on people who wear braces and are embarrassed to smile.

Hugging Day — Hugging could lead to kissing which could lead to petting which could lead to sex which can only lead to yet another political scandal that will destroy the morals of our children.

National Hot Dog Month — You don't need to be Sigmund Freud to figure this one out.

Weights and Measures Day — Obviously an insult to the calorically challenged amongst us.

Soup Month — Most people eat soup with crackers and crackers is a phrase that can mean someone is nuts, so Soup Month may be offensive to people who are nuts.

Nurses' Day — Nurses often see people naked so by celebrating Nurses' Day are we not just advocating public nudity.

Notary Public Day — Public is only an "L" away from being a dirty word, so let's not take any chances.

National Apple Month — A person giddy with merriment from Apple Month festivities could bite into an apple and crack a tooth forcing them to go to a dentist when they are unable to afford dental insurance so this particular holiday discriminates against the uninsured.

MARY E. HIRSCH

Inventors Day — Do you realize that someone had to invent guns, bombs, missiles and Beanie Babies? Is this really something we want to embrace?

Dictionary Day — There are dirty words in the dictionary, I should know I've highlighted them all. We will not be forced to celebrate profanity.

Soon the only day we'll be able to celebrate will be National I Object To Everything Day, unless, of course, someone objects.

URANUS STINKS!

The fields of astronomy and space exploration will be better off when we face the fact that one of the planets in our solar system has a funny name. No it's not Pluto (the dog came after the planet, although ABC's news division will deny it). It's Uranus and it's the butt of constant joking.

Uranus is to science what proctology is to medicine. There isn't a teacher, professor, planetarium narrator, or librarian who doesn't cringe when saying the "U" word. Even if they pronounce it 'Yur-ahhhhhhhh-nus,' everyone knows its 'Yur-anus.' Let's face it, Walter Cronkite couldn't say Uranus without creating one or two snickers from those around him.

The planet's name was originally Georgian, chosen by the man who discovered it —William Herschel. An amateur astronomer, Herschel's discovery was made March 13, 1781 in the garden of his home in England. (He was born Friedrich Wilhelm Herschel, but when he moved from Germany to England he used the name William. Folklore has it that in the 18th century the name "Friedrich," when translated into English, was "Geeky little blond boy who can't find his way out of the forest.") Herschel's discovery was a major event.

If Herschel made his discovery today he'd be hired as the *National Enquirer's* Astronomer To The Stars, have a 1-900 number, and go on tour with Yanni. But back in the 1700s things were a little different. Herschel was made Astronomer to King George III, and moved to Windsor. The Astronomer Royal at this time, Nevil Maskelyne, wrote a letter of congratulations to Herschel stating "I hope you

MARY E. HIRSCH

will do the astronomical world the favor to give a name to your planet, which is entirely your own, and which we are so much obliged to you for the discovery of." Notwithstanding his participles dangling all over the place, Maskelyne opened a big can of worms with this "Name the Planet" idea. Having never taken a management class, Maskelyne didn't know that one person can't make a decision. There must be committees, subcommittees, and sub-subcommittees leading to meetings, lunches, and conferences, resulting in focus groups, overheads and presentations. Finally, the planet's new name would be announced during the Super Bowl and its theme song would be sung by Whitney Houston, Sting, or Garth Brooks.

Herschel wanted to name the planet 'Novum sidus Georgianum' in honor of his boss King George III. Once you see what a brown-noser Herschel was, the name Uranus starts to make sense. Herschel's friend, William Watson, suggested this be modified to 'Georgium Sidus.' Herschel liked it and always referred to the planet as such while others called it "the Georgian Planet" or "the Georgian." But other nations weren't excited to have to look up at a planet named after King George. It would be like wishing on the Stalin Star or being told that tonight Mussolini is aligned with Hitler.

The naked-eye planets had been named after Olympic gods so when this new planet was discovered two names were proposed. Johan Elert Bode suggested 'Uranus' who was the father of Saturn and therefore the supreme Olympian (until Bruce Jenner came along). Of course there is the rumor that Johan Elert Bode is really Jethro E. Bodeen of "Beverly Hillbillies" fame and he was simply trying to spell "Your Highness" when he made the suggestion. Jean Bernouilli, of the Berlin Academy, proposed 'Hypercronius' meaning 'above Saturn.' But who was going to listen to some guy named Jean!

The French wanted to call it Herschel but, not surprisingly, quickly surrendered the idea. Another astronomer, Anders Lexell, wanted to name it 'Neptune.' After much discussion, and reading countless Naming Your Planet Books, it was decided to name the next planet Neptune if it was a boy and Melissa if it was a girl. Someone else suggested 'Cybele,' one of Saturn's wives, but since the planet didn't have multiple personalities, or bleached blond hair, it never caught on. In fact, Uranus was called by different names until 1850 when the *Nautical Almanac*, which is like the Congressional Record of the solar system, replaced "the Georgian" with "Uranus." Perhaps the stars had forewarned of the George Bush administration since it seemed that the two names were interchangeable.

So what should we name this planet? Urpenis and Urvagina can pretty much be ruled out. I wouldn't mind Georgian but you know if the planet is named after an English monarch all the tabloids will report that Princess Di has been sighted on Georgian disco dancing all night long with John F. Kennedy, Jr., Elvis and Jimmy Hoffa. No, we need to find just the right name.

We could name it Congress. After all it takes Uranus 84 years to orbit the sun which is also about how long it takes for Congress to accomplish anything.

It has 15 satellites and no sign of life so if it had some flashing yellow lights and a Detour sign it could be named Road Construction Crew.

MARY E. HIRSCH

The rest of the solar system seems to be dominated by Greek and Roman Gods. Maybe we should name it after some modern day gods like Cash, Looks, Sports, Fame or Wonder Bra. We could name it after a modern hero such as Gandhi, King (Martin Luther, not Larry or Billie Jean), Churchill, Roosevelt, or Bart Simpson.

NASA could probably fund its space program by following the lead of city governments which, for large sums of money, sell businesses the right to put its name on the city's sports facilities. We could sell the name of the planet to the highest bidder. Imagine late at night taking your children into the backyard and pointing out Microsoft or Mitsubishi or Tampax.

Please join me in this effort to return to the scientific community the respect and dignity it deserves. Write to your elected officials and tell them Uranus Stinks!

Real Women Sports

I graduated from high school in 1972. That was also the year Title IX (the federal law that requires schools to give boys and girls equal access to sports) took effect. In the past years there has been great debate about both events — many people says it is a waste of money to invest in sports for girls and many people say my graduation had more to do with getting me out of the building than with my scholastic abilities.

They are wrong about sports for girls. I could see this as I sat in a packed gymnasium at my alma mater watching my niece Britta and her friends take part in the match between the girls' volleyball teams of Southwest and South High. The largest crowd I ever saw for a girls' sports event in 1972 was cheerleading tryouts. It was the blondes vs. the brunettes and the loudest cheer was for a bouncing bosom, not a great block at the net.

Many people credit the success of women at the Olympics to Title IX because it gave those athletes an equal chance for training. Yet, despite the positive effects of the Title IX program, there are still critics. One of the main arguments by these critics, especially at the college level, is that women's athletic teams don't make money. Fool that I am, I thought the purpose of college scholarships, athletic or otherwise, was to help students get an education. If the purpose of college athletes is to make money, why not just send them to the airport and freeway off-ramps to sell flowers, incense, and hand guns?

The other argument is that funding is wasted on women participating in sports where the skill level of men is considered superior (i.e. spitting at umpires, head-

Mary E. Hirsch

banging referees and adjusting genitalia). They suggest
that funding should be limited to events where women can
excel (i.e. giving birth, developing breasts and figure
skating).

How do we compromise on this issue? Do we start
funding new organizations like the WWF (World Washing
Federation) where contestants compete to see whose wash
is the softest, fluffiest, cleanest and brightest? Or how
about the NHL (National Housekeeping League), where
athletes race up and down the floor with vacuum cleaners
or mops to see which team will earn the coveted White
Glove? And every spring how about March Madness when
the NBA (National Bedmaking Association) meets at the
Final Floor. From cots to canopies, these jocks make sure
that their team's sheets don't wrinkle, that their corners are
square and their dust ruffles hang even. And, after winning
the Pillow Fluffing championship, what will our winners do
next? Why, they're going to Slumberland!

When it comes to equality in athletics, let's
remember that we all put our sports bra on the same way,
one cup at a time.

Roberta: A Soap Opera

Roberta. That worried woman. Roberta. Who stared out the window, wondering where was her twin brother Robert? Robert. The one with the BMW, the corporate presidency and the testicles. Where was he? A bird landed on the window sill and began to sing a cheery tune. "Shut up!" Roberta shouted. The bird darted off into the sky. How could the poor little creature have known it was only the PMS talking and not Roberta? How could it have known that Roberta once had had dreams like every other human? How could that bird have known that the car window it just defecated on was Roberta's? (Apparently that bird, now grinning and chirping a revengeful tune, knew much more than we gave it credit.) How could it have known about David?

David. The mechanic who skillfully tuned Roberta's car and realigned her heart. David. A man so secure in who he was that it didn't bother him to wear a shirt embroidered with the name "Bob."

Bob. David's dead partner. Bob. Who died mysteriously from 12 gunshot wounds to the head when he was found in the garden under the window of the bedroom David shared with his wife Natasha.

Natasha. The vixen. Natasha. She used to be a Dancer, then a Prancer but due to reindeer politics and sexist hiring practices she now was a Vixen. Natasha. A hot blooded, near-sighted, East European vixen who played David like a squeaky accordion. Natasha who thought she had shot David when she found him in bed with Bob. But, in reality she had shot Bob who, in a rush to dress before being discovered, put on David's mechanic shirt causing

Mary E. Hirsch

Natasha to believe she shot David. Now David can never again wear his own shirts for fear that Natasha will catch on. But Natasha, being a vixen and all, sensed there was trouble. Trouble in Paradise.

Paradise. The hair removal salon and bakery. Paradise. Where between electrolysis sessions Natasha would bake loaf after loaf of her special oat bran water chestnut bread. Natasha was a vixen, an electrologist and a skillful baker. But her kneads could only be met by Carl.

Carl. The owner of Paradise. Carl, who waxed poetic when he told women "I'm Carl. If you play your cards right you can have a slice of Paradise tonight." Carl, who always carried samples of his bread with him which accounted for his bulging pockets and crumby personality. But one night Carl spoke this line to the wrong woman. Anita.

Anita. The cross-dresser. Anita, the feminine side of truck driver Antonio who had turned the head of Carl. Yet Anita had a complex. But his/her dermatologist cleared that up. Now, good looks was his/her cross to bear. But Anita was not happy. His/her complex was rearing its ugly blackhead and he/she knew he/she would have to return to his/her dermatologist -- the only man who knew him/her for what he/she was, the only man who saw through his/her facade. Dr. Lance Alot.

Lance. Once the pride and joy of his parents. Lance. Replaced in his parents' lives and hearts by a big screen TV and easy to program VCR. Lance, whose broken heart burned for revenge, ended a promising career as a reputable dermatologist to enter the sleazy world of video rentals and liposuction. Lance, who operated a chain of Flab and Film Stores. Lance, whose goal was to own all the movies in the world and then refuse rental privileges to his parents. Lance, whose plan was going well until the store door opened and back into his life walked Bridgett.

Bridgett. The woman with cellulite that could make any doctor forget his professional ethics. Bridgett. The only wrinkle in Lance's medical career. Bridgett. The one woman who could make Lance give-up his video/ liposuction madness. Bridgett. The only woman Lance had cared about since Phyllis.

Phyllis. That love kitten, that wild animal, that passionate pussy. Phyllis. Lance's faithful calico who could spew a fur ball across an entire room. Why did she have to dart out onto the freeway that fateful night? Dart out into the path of Robert's BMW where she was flattened, making Robert late to meet his twin sister, Roberta.

Roberta. That worried woman. . . .

MARY E. HIRSCH

You can always tell when the board of directors are meeting.
I know. There's a definite scent of testosterone in the air.

BRIDGING THE GENDER GAP

The gender gap is always a factor in elections. And it's not surprising when you listen to how the candidates talk: "I'm the quarterback of this team"; "It's fourth and long but we're going to go for it"; "It's time to rally the troops"; or "We're going to go into the trenches to win this election."

Political speeches often use sports or military analogies, and let's face it, military and sports have long been considered men's domains. So why don't male politicians who are trying to bridge the gender gap use analogies that are more female-oriented such as:

- "Thanks to the economic policies of the other party, today's family budget is as tight as a mammogram."

- "Senator Smith has no backbone. When it comes to voting on issues he's like an unfertilized egg; he just goes with the flow."

- "My opponent is trying to force a size 10 idea on a size 14 world."

- "When it comes to delivering on his promises, Senator Jones is all placenta and no baby."

- "A vote for my opponent is as big a waste as a pair of pantyhose on a one-legged man."

- "The senator's background smells as fresh as an overflowing diaper pail."

MARY E. HIRSCH

- "In our search for the truth we will dig deeper than a bra strap on Dolly Parton."

- "Another four years of Senator Thompson has all the appeal of another four years of hot flashes."

- "Trying to get a truthful answer from my opponent is like climbing Mount Everest in a new pair of high heels."

- "If elected, I will be as careful with your money as you are with a bikini wax."

- "Government today needs a good dose of liposuction."

- "Understanding his economic plan is as easy as changing a baby on a roller coaster."

- "Sending Representative Smith to Congress is as futile as putting carrots in your kid's lunch bag."

- "My opponent's record may look clean, but there are dust bunnies under his bed."

- "The opposition's platform has all the charm of ironing a pleated skirt."

- "When it comes to representing the people, Representative Jones is fluff and fold."

- "That party's bandwagon is nothing more than a carpool from hell."

- "Having him in Congress is as frightening as having a sister-in-law who sells Tupperware."

- "When it comes to progress, he's a tampon without a string — stuck in one place."

- "Taxes are like Pap smears—unwelcomed but necessary."

- "The only line longer than my opponent's line of baloney is the one outside a women's restroom at a sports arena."

- "His agenda has so many wrinkles it would take a gallon of cellulite cream to smooth it out."

- "Government is too big. It's time we take the socks out of its brassiere."

At the very least it would be nice if politicians used more realistic male analogies that the entire population can relate to such as "My opponent's political promises will last as long as a six-pack on Super Bowl Sunday."

MARY E. HIRSCH

"Look who's making a person out of himself!"

Back In The Saddle Again

When I was "coming of age" the guys in my circle of friends (a/k/a click) went to the mailbox on their 18th birthday with great trepidation — this could be the day the draft notice arrived. "Greetings" it started, and ended with one terrified boy wondering what the heck he was going to do to get out of this. They all wanted a job — not an adventure. With the arrival of spring, I am now the one who approaches my mailbox with a certain amount of caution. No I don't think Uncle Sam wants me, the medical profession wants me. Yes, it is the time of year when I will be getting "THE CARD." You know the one — white, neatly folded over once and stapled — it's my annual notice:

Greetings: It's been almost a year since you've had a cold steel medical device invade your vagina and scrape away at your cervix. Please call today for an appointment.

Yes, it's Pap time.

Now, I'm the first person to hop on the medical band wagon when it comes to women's health. But just because it's serious business doesn't mean it has to be taken seriously. For instance, it would be nice to get a card that set a lighter tone. Something like:

Perhaps you've been to Maui,
Perhaps you've been to Europe,
Perhaps you have forgotten,
It's time to ride the stirrups

Okay, so no one will turn the card over to see if it's a Hallmark, but at least it's got a little zip to it.

107   Mary E. Hirsch

I would also like it if every doctor performing this exam would stop telling women to relax. Most people find it difficult to relax while laying on a beach listening to the sounds of nature — and this is no beach we're laying on and the only sounds of nature are the rattle of metal and the cries of the circling Medico saying "Scooch, Scooch."

"Scooch" seems to be a favorite way for doctors to tell you to move into exam position I guess it's better than having someone say "Hey, haul your sorry butt down here," or worse yet having your doctor give you those hand signals used by the Navy to guide jets landing on deck. Actually, it would be nice to get a scooch table that had the same gizmo you find at the car wash. When the light turns green you start scooching forward; then when you're in proper scooching position the light turns red. Of course, with the trends in cutting health care costs, it won't be long before you'll see Jiffy Paps popping up all over the place with just such a machine in place.

The other problem I have is being shown a calendar and asked "When was your last period?" I don't know. These are not memorable days for me that I record on my Microsoft Schedule+. When my body becomes bloated, and I start acting like a man, I know what's on the horizon. I still remember having a doctor look me straight in the eyes and ask me "When did you experience the onset of menses?" I thought he was kidding. What was I suppose to do — check my Sisterhood of Menses membership card to see when I crossed over to womanhood? Thinking back on it I guess it's not surprising that this guy thought I'd remember, I'm sure he has the date, time, and object of his first wet dream engraved on a plaque. All I remember was being happy that I now had an excuse to get out of swimming in phy-ed.

This spring, and every spring to come, I will dutifully make my appointment because, despite all my whining and complaining, I know that when it comes to a healthy future I hold the card in my hands. But it sure would be nice if, when it was all over, I could at least get a sucker or a toy or a sticker that says "Be Nice To Me I've Been Scraped."

"I don't know! The last thing he said was "Hey, I'm out of here!"